"The moment I saw the brilliant, proud morning shine high up over the deserts, something stood still in my soul and I started to attend . . ."

D. H. LAWRENCE

Eliot Porter's Southwest

HOLT, RINEHART AND WINSTON · NEW YORK

mr

To my grandchildren

Published by Holt, Rinehart and Winston,
383 Madison Avenue, New York, New York
10017.

Published simultaneously in Canada by Holt,
Rinehart and Winston of Canada, Limited.

Library of Congress Cataloging in Publication Data
Porter, Eliot, 1901–
    Eliot Porter's Southwest.
    1. Photography, Artistic.   2. Southwest, New—
Description and travel—Views.   3. Porter, Eliot,
1901–
TR654.P695 1985   779'.99179   85–13996
ISBN 0-03-006013-3

First Edition
10 9 8 7 6 5 4 3 2 1

Designed by Katy Homans
Printed by Imprimerie Jean Genoud, Lausanne,
Switzerland

Frontispiece: Eagle Nest, New Mexico, 1949

Also by Eliot Porter

In Wildness Is the Preservation of the World

The Place No One Knew: Glen Canyon on the Colorado

Forever Wild: The Adirondacks

Summer Island

Baja California: The Geography of Hope

Galapagos: The Flow of Wildness

Birds of North America: A Personal Selection

Antarctica

Intimate Landscapes

COAUTHOR

Down the Colorado

Appalachian Wilderness

The Tree Where Man Was Born: The African Experience

Moments of Discovery: Adventures with American Birds

American Places

All Under Heaven: The Chinese World

1/21/86

Preface

Eliot Porter has chosen his beloved Southwest as the subject for his first book of black-and-white photographs. Adobe churches, towering cloud formations, mining towns, abstractions of nature, and, especially, the sacred Indian and Spanish lands of Colorado and New Mexico, Arizona and Utah are among the features of this never before collected work made between 1939 and 1965.

Known primarily for a dozen books of color photographs—from *In Wildness Is the Preservation of the World,* which helped to establish the Sierra Club's international reputation, to *Intimate Landscapes,* published to celebrate his landmark exhibition at the Metropolitan Museum of Art—Eliot Porter is also the author of such books as the widely acclaimed and enormously popular *The Tree Where Man Was Born: The African Experience* (with Peter Matthiessen), *Down the Colorado,* and *Birds of North America.*

It was his black-and-white photography, however, that caught the eye of Alfred Stieglitz, who, with Georgia O'Keeffe, gave him his first important show at the prestigious gallery, An American Place, in 1938. A year later, under Beaumont Newhall's curatorship, his black-and-white images were chosen for the exhibition, Sixty Photographs, which inaugurated the Museum of Modern Art's gallery of photography. In that year Dr. Porter, then a thirty-eight-year-old medical scientist at Harvard, switched careers, making photography his full-time occupation.

Porter's artistry with the large-format camera reveals an uncanny ability to select and capture on film the essence of a subject that is more memorable and striking than the larger reality from which it was taken. "The big view," he once said, "conveys less information about the quality of a subject—the forces that shaped the Western landscape—than does close focusing on a particular rock, eroded cliff, or gnarled tree trunk."

Writing recently of Glen Canyon (later flooded to create Lake Powell), Porter was reminded that what he saw when he focused his camera on the details of its sculpted sandstone "evoked visions of thundering torrents, brown with silt and sand, carried down the side canyon from the desert above during the wet period of the last continental glaciation."

It is Porter's concern with the intimate details of nature, his miniaturization of the world, that gives his work its special power and appeal. The Southwest captured here is unique and unrepeatable, especially because many of the scenes recorded have been altered during the past half century. As chronicler and interpreter, he passes on to the viewer impressions left by nature on a changing and timeless land. Weston Neff of the Getty Museum comments on Eliot Porter's photographs: "The mood flows from one of intense concentration on carefully framed details to a meditation on the cosmos, thereby bringing us one step closer to understanding."

—THE EDITORS

An Early View of the Southwest

I was born at the beginning of the century in a house my father built on a bluff overlooking Lake Michigan in the village of Winnetka, Illinois. Events I can recall of those early years are hazy and fragmentary, random images with little emotional content: a toy sheep left out in the rain and ruined, or the memory at age four of being pulled out from under the upstairs hall sofa, where I was hiding from the family doctor. There was one event I can clearly place in time. I was standing by my mother's chair in the living room, which we called the library. There were other women there for tea. One of them asked my age, and either I or my mother said I was six.

Six was the age when school began. My first school was a one-room red house west of the tracks on the south side of North Avenue, the dividing line between the two districts of our village, Winnetka proper to the south and Hubbard Woods, where we lived, to the north. The schoolhouse at that time seemed a good distance west of the

Northwestern Railway tracks, on which Father commuted to Chicago.

With no internal plumbing, the schoolhouse had two outhouses in the back yard—one for girls and one for boys. A blackboard extended along one side wall of the schoolroom, and at the back, on a raised platform, were the teacher's desk and chair and the place where we stood for our recitations. These were terrifying experiences. We were required to recite our pieces before the whole school, standing beside the teacher on the platform. I remember one occasion when a frightened little girl became speechless and, losing control of her functions, wet the floor with a large puddle that flowed under the teacher's chair. The child was excused, but except for that moment the teacher sat impassively, only raising her feet to the rungs of her chair, away from the flood. It was an awesome sight that made a tremendous impression on me and my male schoolmates.

Apparently my parents considered the educational standards of this school inadequate for their oldest son, and after

a year I was transferred to a private boys' school, pretentiously called The College School, in the next suburb. Discipline was strict. Misbehavior, inattention, or stupidity was punished by slaps with a ruler or by standing the culprit in a corner with a dunce cap on his head. I was rescued from this purgatory by an attack of appendicitis that started with a stomachache one morning after breakfast. I must have become quite sick, since I was put in my mother's bed, where I eventually fell asleep, to be awakened by the application of an ether cone over my nose and mouth by our kindly old family physician, Dr. Hooper, who gently urged me to breathe deeply. The operation was performed on the kitchen table and I awoke in the guest room at night, desperately thirsty. To relieve my thirst, a night nurse was instructed to administer small lumps of ice to the inside of my throat, which proved inadequate. Following my recovery, my parents, having reconsidered my educational future and the relative merits of public versus private education, decided in favor of the former and sent me to the town school in Winnetka.

A short distance west of the little red schoolhouse, North Avenue ended at a strip of marshland that extended north and south for many miles. It was called the Skokie, the Indian word for "marshland." West of the marsh lay open farming country, cultivated fields, and woodlots. Much of this area has since been built over by suburban development. The marsh has been drained and a strip along its western edge converted into a parkway that winds along rolling, filled land planted with hawthorn trees and ornamental shrubs. Not until one goes farther west beyond the northbound interstate highway out of Chicago are farmlands still to be found.

The Skokie was a place of mystery and adventure that my friends and I frequently bicycled out to. We would wade out through the marsh grasses to the cattails in deeper water in search of birds' nests and turtles, frogs and snakes. There were birds aplenty: American bitterns, sora rails, red-winged blackbirds, and marsh wrens. To find a bittern's nest was always the most exciting of discoveries. The large buff eggs on a mat of reeds, from which the parent bird had silently and unseen crept away at our noisy approach, was a sight that gave me intense and inexplicable pleasure. We never intended to do harm to any living thing, for we had been taught to respect the mystery and variety of life and would leave our discoveries untouched. Nevertheless, our eagerness and curiosity probably did cause some disruption. My interest in birds developed early and soon became a passion. I kept track of all the nests I found, and after the young had fledged, sometimes there would remain an unhatched, infertile egg, which I took for my cherished birds' egg collection.

An event that made a tremendous impression on me was the return of Halley's comet in 1910. I was eight years old and remember being awakened and led or carried to the backstairs hall window to see the comet. My father, who was scientifically inclined and took an interest in all astronomical events, made sure that his children witnessed this rare occurrence. I will never forget that sight. There it was, an enormous white plume low across the western sky above the black trees. From a glowing, fuzzy coma spread a long, widening, curving tail.

Inspired by my father's excitement about this spectacle, my parents gave a dinner party to celebrate Halley's return, to which they invited many of their Winnetka friends. To dramatize the occasion Father had a large rocket launched from the beach below the house at the moment the guests were gathered on the east porch overlooking the lake. They seemed delighted by the show, with the exception of a late-arriving lady who was coming up the drive below the house just as my father's rocket soared skyward in a burst of flame. She fainted. Mother was contrite about this episode because she felt the guests should have been forewarned.

In those days, before I knew anything of the vast world beyond, my unexplored and untamed West was the Skokie marsh. I felt free there, alone with the birds and the wide-open sky. A few years later the West and its wilderness acquired a more generous meaning when my sister, younger brother, and I were taken by our parents on a camping trip to the Grand Canyon. We camped out by a spring about halfway down the canyon while provisions and tents were packed down on mules, and then spent the next several days exploring the sandstone benches before hiking down to the river. One day we stayed in camp with the cook while Father and Mother went on a walk alone. Close by camp we discovered in an overhead ledge a cave we were able to climb into; hidden there we found what we thought were some old rope and pieces of candles, all of which we threw down to show our parents when they returned. Father was horrified and told us that what we had been playing with were pieces of fuse and sticks of dynamite cached there long ago by a prospector who never returned. I later learned that old dynamite has a tendency to become unstable and explode when roughly handled.

In 1912, when I was ten years old, we were again taken on a camping trip, this time to the Yoho Valley in the Canadian Rockies. Father had camped in the Canadian Rockies before, first as a young man during his college years, and later with Mother and their close friends. He was an enthusiastic amateur mountain climber but attempted no difficult first ascents. He did, however, explore some remote regions of the Rockies and gave names to several peaks and lakes, names that were later accepted by the Canadian government.

Photography was also a hobby of his, for which he used a large, folding Eastman-Kodak. His pictures taken on these camping trips have been preserved in several large photo albums. My interest in photography, encouraged by my father, began at about this time, when I was given a box Brownie, superseded, as my interest in photography developed, by a Kodak.

When I was in high school, we were again taken west, this time to southern Alaska, returning through British Columbia and Alberta, where we camped in Jasper Park. The trip to Alaska was by steamer from Seattle through the inner waterway along the Pacific Coast to Skagway, and by rail to Atlin in Yukon Territory, where gold had been discovered in 1898.

I was determined to go west on my own, to see the land of Lewis and Clark and the Oregon Trail, to see the West that the Forty-niners had seen, and to experience at firsthand the appeal and romance of the vast wilderness lands and mountain ranges that lay beyond the plains.

A close boyhood friend had inspired my resolve. He had dropped out of Cornell and had taken to the road, hitching rides with truckers and hopping freight trains. He joined the horde of migratory workers that in the twenties followed the labor market from the wheat fields of the Dakotas to the lumber camps in Oregon. He worked on the harvests in the prairie states before the days when manual labor was completely replaced by the great combines, and he secured jobs as a swamper in the lumber camps of the Northwest. He worked with road crews and on the railroads, and he traveled all over the West, wherever his fancy guided him. I envied the freedom he enjoyed, and resolved to experience at least a taste of it.

The opportunity came in 1922, at the end of my sophomore year in college, when my sympathetic parents contributed to the purchase of a Model-T Ford at a cost of less than three hundred dollars. In this machine my roommate, Nathaniel Fairbank, and I, with a classmate, Delafield DuBois, planned to spend the summer driving west. We had no definite destination, although we hoped to get jobs for a time in one of the national parks. The Ford was a touring-car model with a fabric top that could be folded down, and had removable isinglass side curtains. The engine was started by a crank that projected forward under the radiator, but before cranking the spark was retarded to avoid a kickback that could break the starter's arm. The most modern feature of the car, demountable rims, made changing tires, a frequent necessity, easier than having to pry them off the wheels in position on the vehicle. The car had four doors, front and back seats, and running boards between the front and rear fenders. Since Ford touring cars had no trunks, the running boards served as a storage place for most of our emergency equipment. One running board held the spare tire, a toolbox, jack and tire tools, a shovel, and an ax. On the other side three cans containing spare gasoline, oil, and water were mounted in a frame attached to the running board and held in place with straps. The cans were of the same rectangular shape, differing only in width. The gas can, painted red, held five gallons; the water can was white and held two gallons; and the third, holding one-half gallon of oil, was blue. As I remember, odds and ends were stashed in a space behind the rear seat. We had a tent, sleeping bags, a cookstove, and provisions, as well as our personal baggage, which pretty well filled up the back of the vehicle.

A Model-T Ford was a remarkably simple mechanism. The planetary transmission was operated by three foot pedals, one for low range, one for reverse, and a brake. The pedals tightened bands on drums; there were no gears as in modern automobiles. A hand-brake lever was used for parking and emergencies. Another hand lever put the car in motion forward. A bar projecting from the right side of the steering column advanced or retarded the spark; a bar on the left side was the throttle for controlling the supply of gasoline. The gasoline tank was located under the front seat, from which fuel flowed by gravity into the carburetor. There was no fuel pump. As a consequence of this system, on very steep grades gasoline could not flow forward to the engine; therefore, in order to negotiate steep hills, the car had to be turned around and backed up, thus putting the gas tank above the level of the engine. Most repairs to a Model-T engine were simple, requiring a minimum of tools and spare parts. A spare distributor cap cost somewhat under two dollars. Other repairs could be taken care of with a screwdriver, monkey wrench, some wire, rubber bands, and friction tape. Tires were, however, a more serious problem. All tires in those days required inner tubes, and the recommended pressure was seventy-two pounds. The treads, which were not as tough as those on today's tires, were easily punctured by sharp objects such as broken glass. Because of the high pressure tires tended to blow out on rocky roads, and their repair became a frequent necessity, for which we kept on hand a supply of inner-tube patches and casing boots.

From Cambridge, Massachusetts, I drove home alone to Winnetka, stopping only to eat and buy gasoline. Somewhere in Indiana, exhausted, I pulled over to the side of a country road, climbed a fence into a field, crawled into my sleeping bag, and promptly fell asleep. I was awakened at dawn by heavy thumping sounds and strange gruntings. On opening my eyes I saw the huge shapes of a herd of Poland China hogs, which out of curiosity had surrounded me during the night.

With Nathaniel and Delafield, I drove north through Wisconsin into Minnesota and turned west to South Dakota. The roads were unpaved graded gravel or dirt except for short stretches out from the larger towns. The interstate highway system was then only in the early planning stage. Roads followed section lines in a rectangular north-south and east-west grid, and would end at right-angle junctions, so that our route became a series of jogs to the north or south until we encountered another western road. Western Minnesota and South Dakota were part of the long-grass prairie, uncultivated and unfenced, green and lush with June wildflowers. We pitched our tent one evening in tall grass on rolling country, and were immediately attacked by swarms of giant, voracious mosquitoes. Without lingering over supper we sealed ourselves in the tent; before we could sleep we had to kill every mosquito inside.

Our route took us through the Black Hills of South Dakota, which I remember particularly for a vein of rose quartz we discovered in an outcrop by a road cut. From the Black Hills we continued on west into Wyoming. As we approached a town somewhere in eastern Wyoming, we picked up a cowboy who was thumbing rides. Recognizing us as eastern tenderfeet, he regaled us with stories about rattlesnakes and how they would crawl into your sleeping bag at night for warmth. When this happened, he told us, you should get out before the snake could attack, which, he explained, would not be difficult, because rattlers can't strike inside the bag.

Our first destination was Yellowstone National Park, which we entered from the east. After seeing the sights for a day or two, we inquired about getting jobs and were told to apply at park headquarters. There we were signed up and sent to separate locations.

I was assigned to roadwork on the Cook City road. The Model-T was parked in the care of the Park Service. Beside the boss, the road crew consisted of four boys, two brothers about my age, me, and an older, more worldly young man whose conversation was mostly about whores. The boss was a much older man who probably operated under contract with the Park Service. His wife was the cook, and their young son did the chores about camp. We slept in Park Service tents but provided our own bedrolls. Meals were served at a wooden table with attached benches set up under a tarpaulin. The road was being graded by horse-drawn scrapers, and since I had no experience driving horses, I was set to work digging out rocks and filling ruts and potholes. After breakfast I would be driven in the boss's pickup with shovel and pickax to places where the rocks were too large for the scraper, left until lunchtime, and picked up again in the late afternoon. One day the boss commended me for my diligence, which my colleagues took as an indication of treachery; I was betraying them by working hard even when the boss was not watching. It was lonely work on a road seldom traveled by tourists, but I enjoyed the solitude.

A herd of buffalo had moved into the valley below our camp, causing the boss considerable anxiety, not on our account or that of the camp, but rather for the safety of the horses, which might stray too close to the herd at night and, being hobbled, could not escape if charged by a bull. A horse can be knocked down by a buffalo and severely injured.

One evening the boss came up to me and asked if I was being treated well. I said I was. His son had told him that the other boys were planning to put cactus in my sleeping bag as a trick to put me, the eastern tenderfoot, in my place. He had intervened and warned them that he would have none of this sort of thing going on in his camp. I never let on that I knew about it. Thus forewarned, I was prepared for a possible confrontation, which occurred one afternoon as we were all returning to camp in the pickup, the four of us in back. I got into a scuffle over some trivial disagreement with the older brother, who grabbed me by my shirt. In the process he fell over the side of the truck and I came over on top of him. He was very mad because he was humiliated by his failure to get the better of me. At this point the boss intervened. "Boys," he said, "fight it out right now and get it over with." But fortunately neither of us wanted to fight, and we climbed back into the truck. Later my opponent admitted he had been trying to tear my shirt off. That evening, after supper, the older boy challenged me to a

WATERFALL. YELLOWSTONE PARK, WYOMING, 1952

wrestling match. It was a fortunate choice for me, since I knew something about wrestling. I put him down, much to his surprise, and I believe the surprise of the boss too. After that I was treated with more respect.

After three weeks on the road gang I decided to see more of the West and asked the boss for my time. He asked me why I was quitting and tried to dissuade me, but I was determined, and explained that I wanted to go on to the Coast. I returned to headquarters with the next supply truck. When I found Nathaniel, he refused to quit; he liked his job and preferred to stay on through the summer. He would return by train. Delafield, however, partly from a sense of obligation but also to be a good sport about it, elected to go on with me.

We drove west into Montana to Butte, and from there followed a route that has become Interstate 90. In the evening about sixty miles beyond Butte, we encountered extensive road repairs where all traffic was diverted through the town of Drummond, and since the construction was a major operation that closed the road, and not soon to be completed, the diversion became known throughout the region as the Drummond detour, a bottleneck for all east-west traffic. It was a bonanza, however, for the people of Drummond who provided lodging for travelers like us, held up at night with no place to camp. We were taken in by a family in town for bed and breakfast.

From Drummond we drove north to Glacier National Park, entering the park from the west, and spent two days walking across the Continental Divide and back from Lake McDonald. We slept in a campsite where tents had been pitched for hikers. That night we were disturbed by an animal making a racket and poking around outside the tent looking for food. John thought it was a bear, but it turned out to be a raccoon. The next day we didn't get back to the ranger station at Lake McDonald until well after sunset. There was a new moon, and the forest was so dark we couldn't see the trail without the flashlight we had forgotten to bring; nonetheless, we managed to keep from straying off into the woods by following the gaps between the trees overhead. When we got back tired and hungry, the ranger took pity on us and let us sleep in a vacant bunkhouse.

In camp one night in the Cascade Range in Washington, I cut my wrist with a hatchet while trimming branches from a spruce sapling for a bow bed. The wound didn't bleed very much, so I tied it up and the next day went to a hospital in Tacoma to be stitched up. The surgeon told me I was lucky that I hadn't severed the radial artery, that the blade had struck the end of the radius, severing a tendon to my thumb. He sewed the tendon ends together, put my forearm in a cast, and sent me on my way, advising me to seek medical aid should my arm become painful. The wound healed without complications, except that the tendon healed to the bone, somewhat limiting the motion of my thumb.

After visiting for a day some friends of Delafield's in Tacoma who tried to persuade me to see another doctor, we drove south along the coast of Oregon and northern California toward the Golden Gate. In California we chose a primitive road south from Eureka that hugged the coast through primeval redwood forests. The narrow dirt track, in places barely wide enough for one vehicle, wound between the trunks of the big trees in a sinuous course that led from high ocean vistas, across damp, fern-shrouded ravines, and back again into the dark depths of the virgin forest. The way was seldom traveled, but would become the coastal route after most of the ancient trees were cut down.

We crossed the Golden Gate by ferry—the suspension bridge had not yet been built—and without spending any time in San Francisco headed east to the Sierra Nevadas and Yosemite National Park. From there we took the road over Tioga Pass into Nevada. We were following the Lincoln Highway, which had been staked out across the most uninhabited parts of the country with red, white, and blue posts. In places the highway was nonexistent. One of these places we came upon in Nevada was a dry lake bed of hard clay that stretched before us endlessly to a distant low horizon. There were no markers, no Lincoln Highway posts to follow on this featureless plain, and no need to steer the car. So we pulled down the hand throttle on the steering post and both of us climbed out onto the engine hood and sat on the radiator with our legs hanging down in front, assigning all responsibility to the mechanical whims of the automobile in a carefree, exhilarating spirit of utter freedom. The car continued for miles at its top speed of forty-five miles per hour in a more or less straight line toward the far shore, which loomed ever higher as we approached until, when we were close to it, we saw that it was barren desert scrub. We found no exit, no car tracks, no Lincoln Highway posts, until we had followed the lake bank for some distance south. At the first sign of civilization, a trading post and gasoline pump, we filled up with gas at the then unheard of price of seventy-five cents a gallon. Until we reached Salt Lake City on a Sunday, the trip was uneventful. As we were driving down the wide main street in the center of the Mormon city a plainclothes detective displaying his badge jumped on the running board and ordered us to pull over. He asked us where we were from and where we were going, and for our drivers' licenses, and then directed us to the police station. In the police station we were questioned again, and Delafield, when asked his age, replied with considerable asperity, "The same as it was ten minutes ago." We were suspected of having stolen the car because it carried Massachusetts plates, and we couldn't produce a bill of sale. To that we replied with irritation, and somewhat arrogantly, that in Massachusetts one is not required to carry around with him the bill of sale for his car, that we did have the registration certificate for the car, and furthermore that, between states, reciprocity agreements covering motor-vehicle regulations assured motorists of reasonable and courteous treatment. The officer, realizing the ridiculousness of his suspicion that we were automobile thieves, felt the need to save face by referring to higher authority. He ordered us to drive him to the home of the chief of police, whom we found in his backyard repairing fishing tackle. After listening to our protestations against the harassment we had been subjected to, he lectured us on the duties of his officers and then dismissed the case against us.

I remember little about the remainder of the drive back to Chicago except for an encounter with a rattlesnake in Nebraska. From Chicago Delafield returned to his home in Connecticut by train. He had had enough of driving, and I, after a few days alone in the empty Winnetka house—the rest of the family was in Maine—drove back to Cambridge.

Two years later, after I graduated from Harvard, the opportunity came to realize my desire to see the American West as my boyhood friend had done, by going on the bum. Father and Mother had planned a tour of England and Norway on which they wanted to take the whole family. I told them I wanted to go west instead, but did not say how I planned to do it, knowing that Father would very much disapprove on the moral ground that to ride freight trains would be to cheat the railroads. I had persuaded a classmate, Francis Birch, who became a famous geophysicist, to participate in the adventure.

For the journey I had made two waterproof canvas sleeping bags, with straps for backpacking, that held blankets, extra clothing, and personal effects. With this minimum baggage, a small sum of money each, and a twenty-dollar bill for emergencies sewed into the fly of our trousers, we set out from Winnetka after my family had departed for Europe. The first stage of the trip was conventional; we paid our fares to Milwaukee on the Chicago and Northwestern. From Milwaukee we went to Oshkosh, but by what means I do not remember, although possibly also legitimately by passenger train. Starting in Oshkosh our mode of travel became surreptitious and extralegal. I seem to remember that we inquired at the railroad station about trains for Minneapolis and St. Paul and were told that a local would be coming through in the evening. Our plan was to catch a Great Northern freight west from Minneapolis because this railroad was reputed to be more lenient toward tramps and migratory workers riding its freights than were the two other lines of the Northwest, the Milwaukee and St. Paul and the Northern Pacific. The reason given for the tolerance was that many Great Northern employees belonged to the IWW, or the Wobblies as they were known, the union of socialist workers dedicated, in theory at least, to overthrowing capitalism.

Our train for St. Paul consisted of coaches and a baggage car for Railway Express and mail. We waited for it on the dimly lighted side of the tracks opposite the station platform. We did not board a coach, but when the conductor gave the all-clear signal to the engineer, who responded with a short blast on the whistle and started the locomotive, we climbed onto the front of the baggage car immediately behind the engineer's tender. A narrow recessed vestibule outside the locked front door provided a place for two people to stand or sit without being conspicuous. This was the traditional way to hitch a ride on a passenger train, and was called riding "blind baggage."

The train rumbled and clattered through the night, puffing smoke and steam. In the early morning it stopped at a water tower to refill the tender's tanks, and the fireman, who had climbed up on top to connect the water spout, saw us and remarked more to himself than to us, "Well, just see all our passengers." He didn't, however, tell us to get off, and soon the train was under way again. The next stop was La Crosse, Wisconsin. By that time we were shivering with cold and had climbed down on the side away from the station and were warming our hands on the cylinder of the locomotive when a railroad detective discovered us and led us into the station, where we were told we would be put in jail unless we paid our fare. We said we had got on at the last stop back, the name of which we happened to remember, and it cost us about a dollar each. The detective

then lectured us about riding passenger trains illegally, but said that we could catch a freight in the yards about a mile down the tracks. There we found a group of switchmen sitting in the sun in front of a freight shed. We told them our story and asked when the next freight train would be coming through. No train would be coming through that day, they said, because it was Sunday, and they advised us to pick up a ride on the highway. They were sympathetic about our predicament, commenting that the railroad dick would get hurt if he treated others as he had us.

On the highway we were very lucky. Before we had walked far, a Pierce-Arrow touring car we flagged stopped and the driver asked where we were going. Minneapolis, we said, and we were invited in; he was headed there too. His wife was with him in the front seat, so we rode in back. During the ride we learned that he was an architect, and we told him what we were doing and how we planned to proceed west from Minneapolis. He dropped us off at the Great Northern railway station, wishing us good luck.

When one sets out to travel by freight train, one does not ordinarily start at the main passenger terminal of a railroad in a major city; instead, the better jumping-off place is the freight yards, where the cars are assembled on the outskirts of the city. What we did, however, was done out of innocence and inexperience. We walked into the station through the main entrance, crossed the lobby to the platform gates, and went out onto a platform. No one accosted us. There were no trains in the station. We went on down to the end of the platform and out onto the tracks, continuing for some distance until we reached what appeared to be freight yards. Eventually we came across a switchman, whom we asked where we could find a freight train going west. He didn't seem particularly surprised by our question, and told us that a freight would be going out that afternoon, that we could recognize it because it would be a long one, and that it would slow down at the last switch. We waited for a long time until finally what appeared to be the right train came by, and then we climbed into an empty boxcar. After a short distance the train stopped, backed up a way, and was still. We were puzzled, but waited until we heard a knocking sound down the line of cars. On looking out we saw a man sealing the doors of the boxcars. He told us the train was going nowhere that night.

By then it was dark, but pretty soon we heard the rumble of another train approaching and saw as it got near that it was pulled by a huge locomotive – not a switch engine – and was made up of many kinds of cars – boxcars, cattle cars, gondola cars, and flatcars. We managed to get into an empty cattle car, not perhaps the best choice, but in the dark we couldn't be choosy. The floor was thickly covered with mostly dried cow dung. We had hoped to find an empty boxcar in which we could spread out our sleeping bags, but in this car that was

out of the question, and we realized we were in for another sleepless night. The best solution we hit upon was to place our packs against one end of the car, where the dung was dry, and then to sleep sitting on them.

The through freights that hauled between the Middle West and the Pacific Coast, for reasons of economy, were made up of approximately one hundred cars, usually of many types, with boxcars predominating but intermixed with gondolas, refrigerators, tank and flatcars, and always a caboose at the end. Freight trains were never hauled straight through, but stopped at all the division points along the main line, which were spaced about every two hundred miles, for a change of crews and engines, and where the grades were steep in the mountains, to couple on another locomotive or even two, one to pull and one to push. Every long freight was made up of cars from many lines—the Santa Fe, Union Pacific, Great Northern, Rock Island, New York Central, Pennsylvania,

Southern Lines, and many others—arranged through reciprocity agreements between the lines to obviate transloading from one line to another. At the division points changes were sometimes made in the makeup of the train, a few cars with local freight being dropped off or added. In these days before the advent of the diesel engine, one of the special distinctions of the railroads was the sound of their locomotive whistles. The Great Northern engines let out a blast, a half-rumbling roar, half-vibrating screech, audible for many miles, that echoed and reechoed from canyon walls.

At the first division point we left the cattle car, found a café near the railway station, and ate a hearty breakfast that cost twenty-five cents. Then we walked out to the end of the yards where all the sidings converged into the main line and waited for our train. At many of these yard ends nondescript bushy thickets bordered the main line on either side, and sometimes the railroad embankment bridged a stream bed or was penetrated by a wide culvert. Migratory workers, hobos, tramps, and bums hung out there while waiting for freight trains. These were the Wobbly jungles romanticized in hobo literature. It was in one of these Wobbly jungles that we first learned about union solidarity. A fellow traveler, recognizing that we were not cast from the same mold as the majority of our companions, and perhaps motivated by compassion to save us from the consequences of our innocence, asked if we had red cards. Red cards, we learned, were certificates of membership in the IWW, passports necessary for riding the freights. Without a card one ran the risk of being rolled by a brakeman—that is, thrown off the train. We were also informed that at the next division point a delegate of the union would sign us up, which in fact is precisely what took place when our kindly adviser introduced us

to a more prosperously dressed older man who sold us our membership cards. The membership card, which I still have, is a small pocket-sized red booklet containing the preamble to the IWW constitution, which begins: ''The working class and the employing class have nothing in common.'' On the next page my name is written and a code for the member who inducted me into the union, followed by date of membership and the industrial department to which I was assigned. My card was dated July 1, 1924, my work class agriculture and farming, and my inductor A4/191. The final pages of the booklet are given over to spaces for monthly dues, stamps, and assessments. I paid dues at fifty cents a month for July, August, and September and fifty cents for an assessment stamp for imprisoned workers. Membership in the IWW was advantageous, however, only on the northwestern lines, where the union was especially strong; not on the central and southwestern or eastern lines, where membership frequently got one into trouble.

At Cut Bank, a division point on the Milk River, a tributary of the Missouri, we were driven off the train by an irate, hard-nosed yard detective who prevented us from reboarding when the train pulled out. In steady rain we holed up in the Wobbly jungle, taking to our sleeping bags to keep dry. After dark the officer went off duty, and we were then able to get on the next freight. From our traveling companions we had heard a rumor that a lumber camp south of Glacier National Park was looking for workers and we decided to try our luck there. We left the train at Belton, west of the Continental Divide, and the first thing we did after finding a secluded place on a creek bank was to give ourselves a long overdue bath and wash our clothes. The next day, a Sunday, we found the camp and were immediately hired. The foreman told us he would put us to work right away, to which we agreed, and he set us to digging a garbage pit. After excavating what we thought was an enormous hole, we were scornfully told it wasn't nearly big enough, and to enlarge it several times.

The camp had only recently opened and to reach more valuable timber was engaged in constructing a logging road. Early the next morning we were assigned to two Swedish lumberjacks as swampers (those who clear brush and trim the branches from felled trees). The lumberjacks were cutting down the largest cedars, trees at least three feet in diameter, and sawing them into sixteen-foot lengths to be used for the construction of a corduroy road. Our job was to split the logs in half. We were provided with axes, wedges, and mauls. Before we could begin the splitting, a tangle of brush and branches had to be cleared, and even though the logs were rotten at the core and easy to split, we were hard-pressed to keep up with the tree-felling.

The camp consisted of a bunkhouse equipped with steel beds, mattresses, and blankets, a cookhouse with an attached eating shed, a commissary, and stalls for horses. As soon as we were installed in the bunkhouse, one of the workers, spotting our packs, advised us not to use our sleeping bags and to stash them out of sight under our bunks because the union, which had long opposed the custom of hiring workers who could provide their own blankets—blanket stiffs—as discrimination against those who couldn't, had recently won an agreement that the logging camps would provide all bedding. The food at the camp was plentiful and good, another victory for the union. For breakfast, the most important meal, we could have as much as we could eat—a choice of hot or cold cereal, eggs with ham or bacon, fresh bread and butter, hashed potatoes, steak, and coffee.

After a week or more of splitting cedar for the corduroy road, which by then had been laid down for a considerable distance into the forest, the next step was to cover the logs with dirt, and we were given new jobs. I was assigned to handle a fresno, a scoop attached to a U-shaped bridle drawn by a horse and used for moving dirt and gravel. Following along behind, the operator controls the scoop with two wooden handles, which are like those on a wheelbarrow. To fill the scoop the handles are lifted, causing the lip to dig into the ground, and when filled the handles are lowered. The scoop is then pulled along the ground to the place where the dirt is to be delivered, and dumped by throwing the handles forward, upsetting it.

One of the loggers, a tough character with a belligerent disposition and a propensity for picking fights at the slightest provocation, had justifiably acquired the reputation of camp bully. Since no one was willing to take him on Francis came forward and offered to box with him. I did not witness the fight, but since it apparently ended in a draw, my friend's standing in the camp, and mine by association, was considerably enhanced. People came up to me after the fight to ask in awe where my friend had learned to box.

We had been in camp a little more than two weeks, still working behind the scoop, when we got fired. The excuse for letting us go was an accident I had with the scoop, which I was dumping at the edge of the corduroy road as directed. As I tripped it, one of the handles caught between two logs and snapped off. By bad luck, the boss happened to be watching. I was sent back to camp for a new handle, and that evening we were given our time. We were paid a little over two dollars a day.

The next morning we walked out of camp to Columbia Falls, about eighteen miles away, where we caught a freight on the Great Northern to Spokane, Washington, and on to Pasco on the Columbia River. There we were thrown off the train and warned not to ride any freight out of that city. Pasco had a reputation among hobos as a bad town, so we walked across on a railroad bridge to the west side of the Columbia River and were able to get on a Union Pacific freight to Auburn, south of Seattle. In Auburn we managed at some risk to board a rather fast-moving train going south, probably a Southern Pacific freight, which we stayed with all the way to Eugene, Oregon, where we were again bumped off.

It was probably then that we decided we had gone far enough, and turned back. We worked our way northeast by rail to The Dalles on the Columbia River, which was then free-flowing before the Grand Coulee or any other western dam had been built. While scouting the freight yards for a made-up eastbound freight, we were accosted by a plainclothes policeman and questioned at length. When we had satisfied him of our innocence of any criminal act, we were informed that the police were looking for two men from Portland wanted for murder. We were then ordered out of the yards. Night overtook us on our way to the highway, and since the chance of hitching a ride was remote, we searched for a sheltered place to hit the sack. The road was bordered by chaparral in which we found a small space of clear ground surrounded by bushes large enough for our sleeping bags. The next morning we discovered we had camped in a thicket of poison ivy, but luckily we were not affected by it.

The rest of the journey is vague and dreamlike, and only a few episodes stand out clearly in retrospect. We traveled on the Northern Pacific across Idaho, all of Montana, and on into the wheatbelt, where the harvest was in full progress and where many of our fellow travelers were headed.

One evening as we came into Montana, the freight we were riding stopped for crew and engine changes at the division point near the small town of Paradise, northwest of Missoula. With the other riders, maybe twenty or more, I went into the railroad station café for coffee and doughnuts, and then returned to the yards to await the train's departure. We hadn't been waiting long before we were rounded up by railroad detectives and herded back to the station because someone had skipped out without paying for his coffee. No one admitted to the crime and we were warned that none of us would be allowed to get back on the train unless the culprit confessed or was caught. While the police searched the yards, we were advised to stay on the platform, and we were told the train would slow down for us as it came through. It was not long before the detectives returned with a shabby, meek man who confessed he had not paid because he had no money. Someone in our group paid for him, and he was let go. Several of the men bawled him out for not asking for help, pointing out that his behavior got them all in trouble and gave migratory workers and other freight-riders a bad name. As promised, the train did slow down at the station, and we continued east.

Somewhere in Oregon everyone on the train, two dozen or more of us, were driven off by a brakeman with a club. I recall especially one train we rode in Idaho that was made up almost entirely of tank cars. There was no safe place to sit, but it was night and we were bone-tired; to guard against going to sleep and falling off we used our belts to strap ourselves to the handrail on the side of a tank car. I also discovered that I could stand on the catwalk and squeeze both arms between the handrail and the tank so that the rail was under my armpits where I could hang securely and sleep.

How we finally got to Chicago and home to Winnetka I don't recall exactly, only that baths and clean clothes were luxuries we had been looking forward to for a long time. Francis returned to Chevy Chase by passenger train, and I stayed in Winnetka until my parents returned from Europe. When I told them what I had been doing, they were astonished and interested. Father did not reproach me for cheating the railroads.

This adventure ended for fifteen years my further exploration of the West. I had graduated from Harvard with a degree in chemical engineering, but my interest had turned from engineering to biochemistry, and in the fall I entered Harvard Medical School, where in my second year I became acquainted with and was greatly influenced by Dr. Hans Zinsser, who headed the bacteriology department. My intention had never been to practice medicine, but to use medical education as a step toward a career in biochemical research. After graduation I obtained a position in the bacteriology department at Harvard as a teaching assistant and later was appointed a tutor and research assistant. During that period my interest in photography revived to become an increasingly important avocation. I photographed on most weekends and intensively during summer vacations, gradually accumulating a large number of prints that were seen and criticized by Ansel Adams and others, and later judged by Alfred Stieglitz, an acquaintance of my younger brother, the artist Fairfield Porter. Stieglitz was unsparing in his criticism, but was also encouraging. Once a year thereafter I would go to New York with a box of photographs to show Stieglitz, who continued to give me kindly advice until one unforgettable day in October 1938, when, after twice looking through what I had brought, he said, ''I want to show these.''

22

My photographs were exhibited by Stieglitz at his gallery, An American Place, for three weeks from December 1938 to January 1939. This event changed the course of my life. I had made no contributions to scientific knowledge, and my prospects for an academic career were fading. It seemed obvious to me that I was a better photographer than scientist, and so I resolved to give up teaching and research for photography, and at the end of the academic year in June did not seek reappointment.

Since I had freed myself from institutional connections, there was no need to stay in Cambridge. I could live wherever my fancy dictated. My wife's brother had moved to Santa Fe, and suggested we come there. This was the West again, but a part of the West I did not know. My wife Aline and I decided to try it. We drove out to Santa Fe in the fall, but it was clear Aline didn't share my enthusiasm for New Mexico and after a year we moved back to my birthplace in Illinois. My interest in the Southwest had

a romantic attraction I could not shake, going back to that childhood camping trip to the Grand Canyon. I returned alone to New Mexico several times to photograph the landscape, the adobe buildings and churches, and the desert birds.

Then World War II changed everything. We moved back to Cambridge, where I accepted a job at the Radiation Laboratory at MIT, helping to develop radar. After the war, Aline became more reconciled to living in the West, and in 1946 we moved permanently to Santa Fe.

The Southwest, from the mid–nineteenth century, when the great western migration over the Santa Fe Trail began, until World War I, was a place of high adventure and romance. Roads were nonexistent and communications difficult. The whole region that comprises much of the four-corner states was then known as the Great American Desert. High, arid country, and formidable still, although much of it has become accessible by road, it is beautiful, desolate country. Geologically a young land, the Southwest allows one to witness the ongoing

process of change almost before one's eyes. The attractiveness of the land can be seen in its sparse beauty, sharp outlines, cleanliness, and, if it is permissible to speak of nature in those terms, its unaffected simplicity.

The Rocky Mountains, which wall off the prairie lands of the Midwest, extend south into northern New Mexico, where they end in the Sangre de Cristo Mountains, which turn red in the evening after sunset, giving them their name. La Villa Real de la Santa Fé de San Francisco de Assisi—Santa Fe—disputes with St. Augustine, Florida, the distinction of being the oldest European city in the United States. It was founded by Pedro de Peralta in 1610 in the foothills on the western end of the Sangre de Cristos at seven thousand feet. It is here that the Great American Desert begins, becoming increasingly arid as it extends westward across the Rio Grande Valley into Arizona and Utah. Here lie the rainbow-hued badlands, Canyon de Chelly, Monument

MONUMENT VALLEY, ARIZONA, 1940

Valley, and the canyon lands of the Colorado River basin. It stretches from the Green River into Cataract Canyon, Glen Canyon, and the mile-deep Grand Canyon.

The Southwest is big, wide land, and by eastern standards sparsely inhabited; people are now streaming in because word has gotten around that the conditions of life are more agreeable here than in the densely populated, polluted districts east of the Mississippi and west in California. Another attractant is the Spanish-Indian culture, with its adobe architecture of flat-roofed, one-story buildings that unobtrusively occupy the semi-arid landscape. The architectural harmony is enhanced by the whitewashed columned portals, paneled doors, and ornate lintels that are common features of many of the houses. Each village and Indian pueblo has its own church, frequently painted white, with its bell cupola, surmounted by a cross, presiding over a graveyard of carved wooden crosses.

So beautiful is the Southwest, so remarkable its unmatched geological features, that its fame is now worldwide. The stimulation of thin air; the intense blueness of the sky; the towering thunderheads of summer that rumble and flash and produce sheets of rain with a sudden rush of water that soon passes, leaving only a wet arroyo to dry within an hour; the quick change of climate, from burning dry heat that allows no sweat to wet one's clothing to a shivering cold during the rainfall; these are among the attributes of a land that gets into one's blood and bones.

Plates

1. KITCHEN WINDOW. TESUQUE, NEW MEXICO, 1961

2. HOUSE AND GATE. NAMBE, NEW MEXICO, 1948

3. ADOBE RUIN AND CORRAL. CIENEGUILLA, NEW MEXICO, 1940

4. RANCH. LA PLAZA, NEW MEXICO, 1948

5. PORTAL. PENASCO, NEW MEXICO, 1940

6. WINDMILL. ANIMAS, NEW MEXICO, 1947

7. CORRAL. LA BAJADA, NEW MEXICO, 1960

8. SYCAMORE TREE. ARIZONA, 1940

9. SANTURIO, CHIMAYO, NEW MEXICO, 1940

10. CHIRICAHUA MOUNTAINS, APACHE PASS, ARIZONA, 1947

11. ADOBE HOUSE. CHIMAYO, NEW MEXICO, 1940

12. MAIN STREET. OURAY, COLORADO, 1948

13. MUSEUM. ASPEN, COLORADO, 1950

14. WELL HOUSE AND DOOR. PENASCO, NEW MEXICO, 1940

15. CITY HALL. TOMBSTONE, ARIZONA, 1940

16. LEADVILLE, COLORADO, 1940

17. CEMENT WORKS. SALIDA, COLORADO, 1945

18. SAGUARO NATIONAL MONUMENT, ARIZONA, 1940

19. ERODED HILLS. BLACK PLACE, NEW MEXICO, 1945

20. MINER'S HOUSE. LEADVILLE, COLORADO, 1948

21. HOUSE AND FENCE. ASPEN, COLORADO, 1950

22. ABANDONED FARM. CLOVERDALE, NEW MEXICO, 1947

23. THE OUTSKIRTS. ALAMOGORDO, NEW MEXICO, 1947

24. RANCH HOUSE ON TOMICHI CREEK, COLORADO, 1948

25. MINE BUILDINGS ON THE WAY TO OURAY, COLORADO, 1951

26. MINERS' HOUSES. SILVERTON, COLORADO, 1951

27. PROFESSOR SCHMIDT'S HOUSE. CERRILLOS, NEW MEXICO, 1940

28. WORKING MINE. MADRID, NEW MEXICO, 1940

29. DETAIL OF CABIN. ANIMAS FORKS, COLORADO, 1958

30. HILLSIDE AND RUIN. ANIMAS FORKS, COLORADO, 1958

31. CANILLE, ARIZONA, 1947

32. STORM OVER SANGRE DE CRISTO MOUNTAINS, NEW MEXICO, 1940

33. RANCH. PECOS RIVER, NEW MEXICO, 1940

34. HYDE PARK. SANGRE DE CRISTO MOUNTAINS, NEW MEXICO, 1947

35. CHURCH. CANONCITO, NEW MEXICO, 1939

36. CHURCH YARD. VELARDE, NEW MEXICO, 1948

37. CHURCH. TESUQUE, NEW MEXICO, 1949

38. CEMETERY. QUESTA, NEW MEXICO, 1948

39. WINDOW OF ADOBE HOUSE. LA BAJADA, NEW MEXICO, 1961

40. DOOR HASP. ALGODONES, NEW MEXICO, 1947

41. HOUSE. TRUCHAS, NEW MEXICO, 1940

42. CHAPEL AND JUNKYARD. LA PLAZA, NEW MEXICO, 1948

43. COLLINS STORE. OURAY, COLORADO, 1948

44. STORE. RANCHOS DE TAOS, NEW MEXICO, 1940

45. BARBER SHOP. MESILLA, NEW MEXICO, 1940

46. POST OFFICE. TRAMPAS, NEW MEXICO, 1940

47. ORTIZ MOUNTAINS, NEW MEXICO, 1940

48. STORM OVER BLACK MESA, NEW MEXICO, 1948

49. GRAND CANYON, ARIZONA, 1940

50. WHITE FORMATIONS. BLACK PLACE, NEW MEXICO, 1948

51. ERODED BENTONITE. HANKSVILLE, UTAH, 1963

52. CHURCH. SILVERTON, COLORADO, 1951

53. WINDOW AND LADDER. TRUCHAS, NEW MEXICO, 1961

54. BARN DOOR. CUNDIYO, NEW MEXICO, 1961

55. CROSS AND CHURCH. CORDOVA, NEW MEXICO, 1961

56. GEORGIA O'KEEFFE WITH BUST BY MARY CALLERY. GHOST RANCH, NEW MEXICO, 1945

57. HORSE SKULL. GEORGIA O'KEEFFE'S HOUSE, ABIQUIU, NEW MEXICO, 1952

58. POJOAQUE, NEW MEXICO, 1950

59. WHITE SANDS, NEW MEXICO, 1947

60. BENTONITE MOUNDS. HEARTNUT DESERT, UTAH, 1963

61. TOWER IN MUMMY CAVE. CANYON DEL MUERTO, UTAH, 1953

62. DOOR. GEORGIA O'KEEFFE'S HOUSE, ABIQUIU, NEW MEXICO, 1949

63. PORTAL. NORTH OF TAOS, NEW MEXICO, 1940

64. HANKSVILLE ROAD, UTAH, 1963

65. CEDAR TREE. GHOST RANCH, NEW MEXICO, 1940

66. FORT UNION, NEW MEXICO, 1940

67. OUTCROP. ARIZONA, 1950

68. GREAT SAND DUNES NATIONAL MONUMENT, COLORADO, 1960

69. DEAD HORSE. ARIZONA, 1940

70. CACTUS. SUPAI, ARIZONA, 1940

71. CROSS. TRUCHAS, NEW MEXICO, 1940

72. DEAD COW. ROAD TO SUPAI, ARIZONA, 1940

73. CHURCH. PLACITA DE TAOS, NEW MEXICO, 1940

74. GRAVEYARD. TESUQUE PUEBLO, NEW MEXICO, 1939

75. CHURCH. CORDOVA, NEW MEXICO, 1961

76. CHURCH. CORDOVA, NEW MEXICO, 1940

77. OAK TREE. LUKACHUKAI MOUNTAIN, ARIZONA, 1950

78. ASH TREE. ARIZONA, 1958

79. NATURAL BRIDGES NATIONAL MONUMENT, UTAH, 1947

80. WHITE HOUSE RUINS. CANYON DE CHELLY, ARIZONA, 1953

81. NEAR MULE CREEK, NEW MEXICO, 1948

82. TENT ROCKS, NEW MEXICO, 1940

83. MUDFLAKES. CANYON DE CHELLY, ARIZONA, 1953

84. ROCK FLAKES ON BENTONITE. BLACK PLACE, NEW MEXICO, 1953

85. FORT UNION, NEW MEXICO, 1940

86. WHITE BOULDER. BLACK PLACE, NEW MEXICO, 1945

87. NORTH OF TAOS, NEW MEXICO, 1948

88. CHAMA RIVER, NEW MEXICO, 1940